Handbook of Stitches

Handbook of Stitches

200 Embroidery Stitches, old and new, with descriptions, diagrams, and samplers

BY GRETE PETERSEN AND ELSIE SVENNÅS

Foreword by Jacqueline Enthoven, author of *Stitches of Creative Embroidery* and *Stitchery for Children*

 VAN NOSTRAND REINHOLD COMPANY
NEW YORK   CINCINNATI   TORONTO   LONDON   MELBOURNE

Van Nostrand Reinhold Company Regional Offices:
New York   Cincinnati   Chicago   Millbrae   Dallas
Van Nostrand Reinhold Company International Offices:
London   Toronto   Melbourne

Printed in the United States of America.
Diagrams by Grete Petersen, with additions by Elsie Svennas
Samplers worked by Lena Nessle, with additions by Elsie Svennas
Photographs by Eric Sjostrom
Published in the United States by
Van Nostrand Reinhold Company
A Division of Litton Educational Publishing, Inc.
450 West 33rd Street, New York, N.Y. 10001
16   15   14   13   12   11   10   9   8   7

Foreword

Recently, my publisher brought to my attention the Danish handbook *Sting og sømme*. After reading it I immediately thought of the pleasure such a compact handbook would give to English-speaking people.

Thanks to Anne Wilkins' competent translation, very few changes had to be made to adapt the handbook. Besides the large number of recorded stitches, what should be particularly valuable to students of embroidery are the examples illustrating the use of stitches, some of them worked in the form of attractive contemporary samplers.

To the pages of *Sting og sømme* we added a few from *Märkbok* giving interesting uses of stitches for monograms and Cross Stitch designs.

Now that it is available in English, I believe this handbook will become just as popular in the English-speaking countries as it already is in Denmark.

JACQUELINE ENTHOVEN

Introduction

For this little handbook, which we hope will be useful, we have selected from among the great variety of stitches and styles in existence those which should prove both enjoyable and practical for the modern embroiderer.

In addition to the better-known stitches we have included the most important of the old styles of work – especially Danish ones – since so much interest is taken today in ancient embroidery. Museums all over the world provide anyone who is interested with the opportunity to study and copy patterns and designs. The photographs in this book will show how a contemporary effect can be obtained by, for example, using variants of the basic stitches.

We have included a complete index of stitches. If the reader cannot recall the name of a stitch or if a stitch is needed for a specific purpose, it can be quickly and conveniently found by simply leafing through these pages, noting the diagrams and the photographs of samplers.

Practical Advice

Perhaps the most important function of embroidery work today is to provide relaxation and the opportunity to exercise one's imagination. The result, however, should also be attractive and durable. The materials and stitches must therefore be wisely chosen, and the work itself carefully prepared and carried out.

The fabric and the threads must be of good quality and com-patible. The thread must be able to slip easily through the cloth, and be able to form the texture the embroiderer has in mind. The needle must be of the right size for the fabric and thread to be used. For traced embroidery, use a sewing needle or a darning needle with a point. A tapestry needle, without a point, is better for canvas or counted-thread work on coarser material. A needle very slightly coarser than a double thickness of the thread to be used in it will be the easiest to work with.

Scissors are important. They should be small, sharp, and pointed. A stiletto is necessary for work in which threads are forced aside to form eyelets.

When choosing fabric for counted-thread embroidery, check the number of threads needed per motif, so that the finished work will be the intended size. For some kinds of work it is also important that the warp and the weft have an equal number of threads per square inch, that is, an inch measured in either direction should contain the same number of threads, otherwise a pattern that is supposed to have the same dimension vertically and horizontally will be distorted.

For drawn-thread and drawn-fabric work, material woven of dyed yarn is best; if it is woven of white yarn and then dyed, the threads will not always be completely even in color throughout. Make sure of this by pulling a few threads from the cut edge.

Fabric to be used in appliqué, or any kind of work in which material is pieced together, should be pre-shrunk and checked for color-fastness.

Squared or graph paper is very useful if a motif is to be enlarged or reduced.

Embroidery to be worked over counted threads follows a

pattern drawn on graph paper. It is helpful to mark the center line and the boundaries of important sections on the grid.

For embroidery on closely woven fabric, the design is drafted on transparent paper. There are various methods of transferring it to the fabric. For instance, carbon-paper can be laid between the drawing and the fabric, after which the design is transferred by tracing firmly with a hard pencil. It is also possible to rub the reverse of the drawing with a soft pencil, as a substitute for carbon-paper. In either case, the fabric must be held smooth and taut and the pattern fastened down. A firm base must be used, and care must be taken not to cause smudging by pressure of the hands.

A better method, but rather more elaborate, is to prick out the lines of the pattern with a needle or a perforating-wheel, using a soft underlay. Spread the fabric over a layer of paper. Place the pricked-out pattern on top. Hold one side firm with weights or any heavy objects – adhesive tape is also a possibility. Moisten a piece of rolled-up felt or foam rubber with oil-paint, thinned down with paint thinners or turpentine. Use blue on a pale fabric, white on a dark, and press the color gently through the holes. The pattern paper can be raised carefully now and then to see whether the design is coming through clearly. If not, another layer of color can be pressed through. If dry powdered color is used, the lines must be worked over with a pencil. Not all fabrics take color equally well, so it is wise to experiment beforehand on a scrap of the material.

For fine work, it is well to use a frame to avoid puckering. Circular frames consist of two rings that fit into each other. The inner ring is laid under the fabric, the outer ring on top. The fabric is stretched and held firmly between the rings by means of screws. Usually this type of frame is small enough to be held by the thumb above and the fingers below. As well as holding the frame firm, this hand raises the fabric just enough to allow the free hand to take the needle down and up through it. There are larger rectangular frames, which hold the fabric stretched by means of wooden rollers. This kind of frame needs to be supported against the edge of a table, or a chair-back, since the work is done with one hand above and the other below the fabric.

Never start with a knot. Some stitches, for example, the Chain Stitch, the Buttonhole Stitch, the Feather Stitch, call for a special method of starting a new thread. (See diagram opposite.) The last stitch made with the old thread is not drawn tight until the newly-fastened thread (shown in black on the diagram) is taken upwards into the loop and completed.

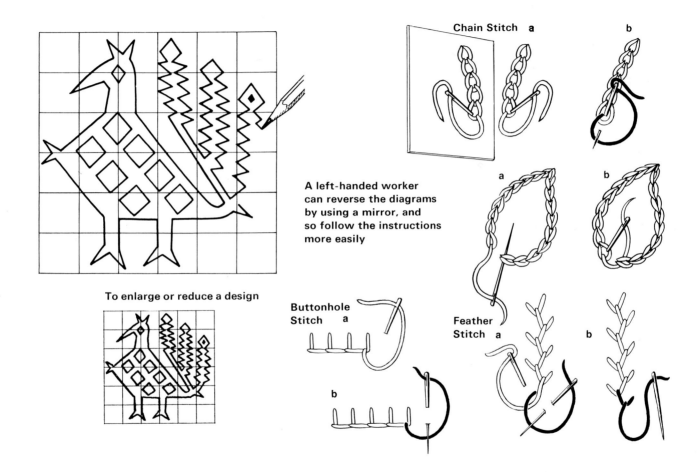

To enlarge or reduce a design

Chain Stitch **a**   **b**

A left-handed worker can reverse the diagrams by using a mirror, and so follow the instructions more easily

a   **b**

Buttonhole Stitch **a**

b

Feather Stitch **a**   **b**

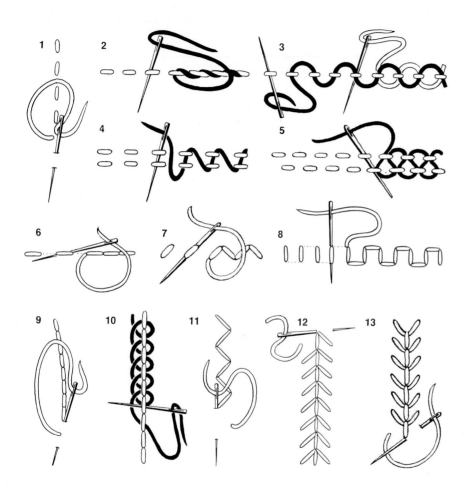

Running Stitch, Back Stitch, Holbein Stitch, Fern Stitch, Fly Stitch

1. *Running*.
2. *Whipped Running* using the same color or a contrasting color.
3. *Threaded Running* using either one or two colors.
4. *Whipping* through rows of Running.
5. *Threading* through rows of Running.
6. *Double Running* or *Holbein Stitch*.
7. *Holbein Stitch* worked diagonally in two journeys.
8. *Holbein Stitch* at right angles, worked in two trips.
9. *Back Stitch*.
10. *Pekinese Stitch*. Back Stitch can also be threaded as in Figure 3.
11. *Arrowhead Stitch*. Back Stitch worked zigzag (compare with Figure 129).
12. *Fern Stitch*. Work the right-hand stitch first, then the center, and finally the left.
13. *Fly Stitch*, worked like Chain Stitch.

This sampler shows the stitches worked partly over counted threads, partly along traced lines

12 11 10 9 8 7 6 5 4 3 2 1 12 1 2 3 4 5 6 7 8 9 10 11 12

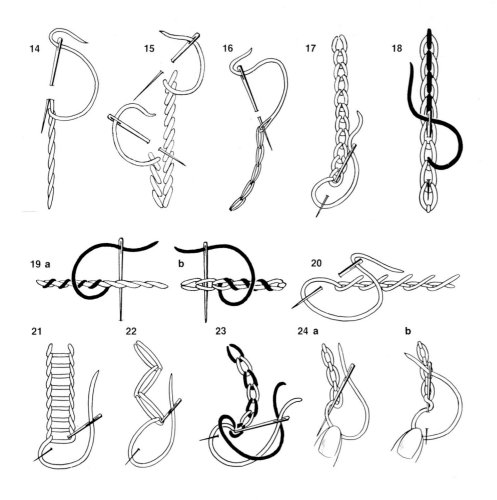

Stem Stitch, Chain Stitch

14. *Stem Stitch* usually worked with the yarn to the right.
15. *Stem Stitch* (canvas) worked from left and right.
16. *Split Stitch* is used both for outlining and as a filling stitch.
17. *Chain Stitch.*
18. *Back Stitched Chain.*
19. *Whipping* over (a) Stem Stitch (in the reverse direction to that of the stitch) or (b) Chain Stitch.
20. *Twisted Chain Stitch.*
21. *Open Chain Stitch.*
22. *Chain Stitch* worked in a zigzag.
23. *Chequered Chain Stitch.* The two colors are worked alternately with the same needle. Can also be worked with two needles.
24. *Cable Chain Stitch.*

The sampler shows the same motifs worked in various ways. In the center, Chain Stitch as a filling, and detached stitches, also called Daisy Stitch. Flowers worked in Daisy Stitch are called 'Mille Fleurs'

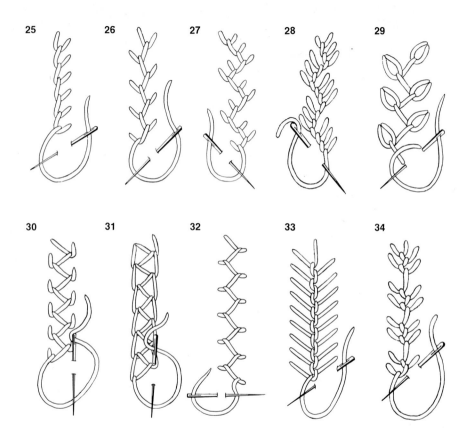

Feather Stitch

25. *Single Feather Stitch.*
26. *Feather Stitch.* One diagonal stitch from each side.
27. *Double Feather Stitch,* with two diagonal stitches on each side.
28. *Multiple Feather Stitch,* with several diagonal stitches grouped on each side alternately.
29. *Feathered Chain Stitch* (*Long-Armed Zigzag Chain*).
30. *Straight Feather Stitch.*
31. *Double Chain Stitch.*
32. *Open Cretan Stitch,* worked with small horizontal stitches.
33. *Long-Armed Feather Stitch* or *Spine Stitch,* worked very closely in to the center.
34. *Feather Stitch* worked in groups.

The Feather Stitches can be worked in regular rows between drawn lines, but this sampler shows how they can be used to fill the spaces between irregularly drawn lines

14

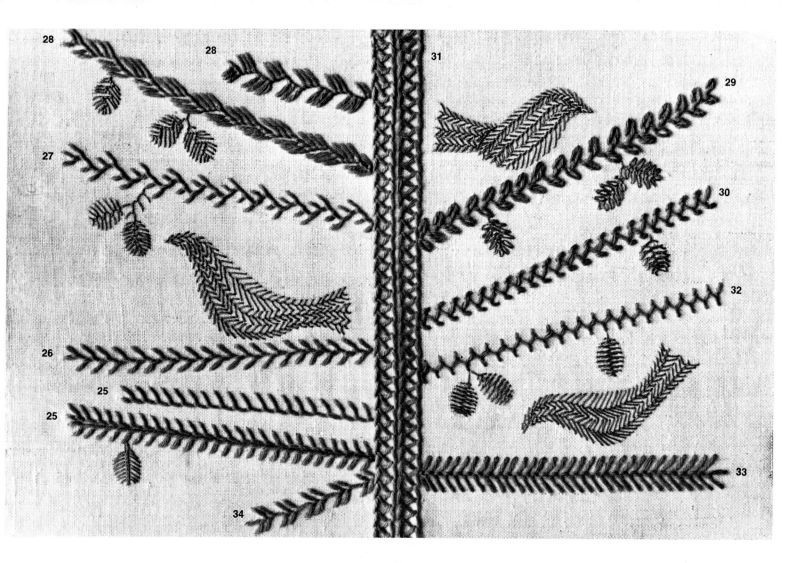

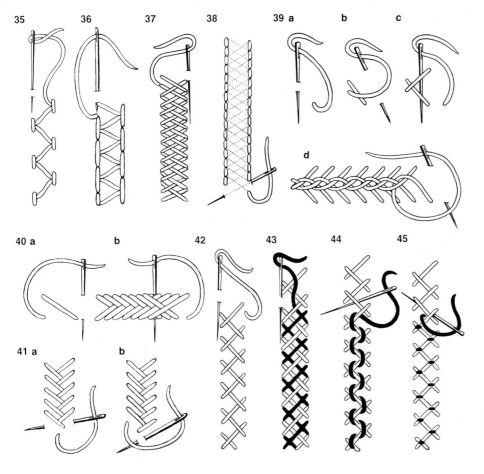

Chevron Stitch, Herringbone Stitch

35. *Chevron Stitch* with small side-stitches.
36. *Closed Chevron Stitch* with continuous side-stitches.
37. *Closed Herringbone Stitch* resembling the reverse of Double Back Stitch.
38. *Double Back Stitch* resembling the reverse of Closed Herringbone Stitch. This stitch can be worked from either side of the fabric. On fine materials, the crossed threads show through.
39. *Vandyke Stitch.*
40. *Basket Stitch* looks similar to a Close Fishbone Stitch, but gives a more raised effect.
41. *Fishbone Stitch.*
42. *Herringbone Stitch.*
43. *Double Herringbone Stitch* in two colors.
44. *Threaded Herringbone Stitch.*
45. *Herringbone Stitch* couched down with small stitches, here in a contrasting color.

Shadow work is done on fabric thin enough to allow the threads on the reverse to show through. Herringbone Stitch is worked either open or closed along double lines drawn on the fabric

16

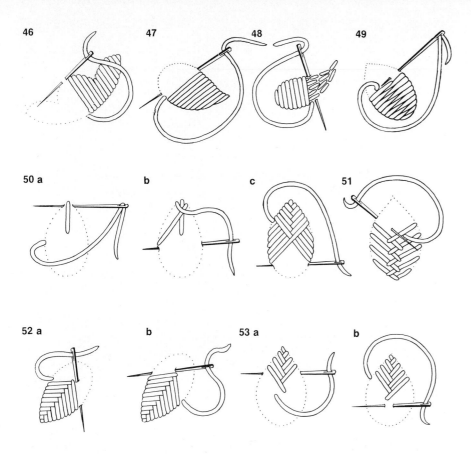

Satin Stitch, Padded Work, and various kinds of Fishbone Stitch

46. *Surface Satin Stitch* occurs in Amager work and in Swedish Delsbo and Bleking work.
47. *Satin Stitch.*
48. *Padded Satin Stitch.*
49. *Flat Stitch,* if the needle is brought up in front of the thread. If it is brought up behind the thread *Close Cretan Stitch* is the result. The Flat Stitch is also made with the needle pointing from inside out.
50. *Raised Fishbone Stitch.* Tailor's Arrowheads are worked in the same manner.
51. *Leaf Stitch.*
52. *Fishbone Stitch.*
53. *Open Fishbone Stitch.*

The sampler shows how the same motif can be filled in various ways. Each branch shows one stitch. Some produce a close or raised effect, others are flatter and others again, open

18

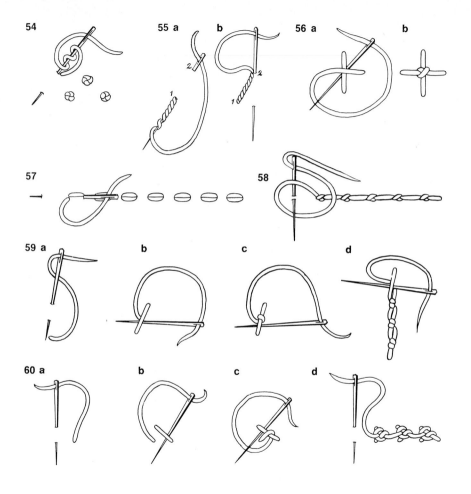

Knotted Stitches

54. *French Knots.* Twist the thread round the needle. Hold the thread taut and insert the needle close to where it last emerged. The more twist of thread round the needle, the larger the knots. They can be used singly or as a filling.

55. *Bullion Knots.* The distance between points 1 and 2 is the length of the knot. Twist the thread round the needle to the desired length, hold the thread taut and reinsert the needle at 2.

56. *Four-legged Knot Stitch.*

57. *Dot Stitch.* Coarse thread and tiny stitches produce a knotted effect.

58. *Coral Stitch* can also be worked zigzag.

59. *Portuguese Knotted Stem Stitch.*

60. *Double Knot Stitch.*

Knotted Stitches give a pronounced raised effect and can, therefore, as in this sampler, be worked in the same color as the ground fabric, although, naturally, they can also be worked in contrasting colors. Care must be taken not to press the work so firmly that the stitches are flattened out. The thread must be held taut, so that the knots formed are firm and even

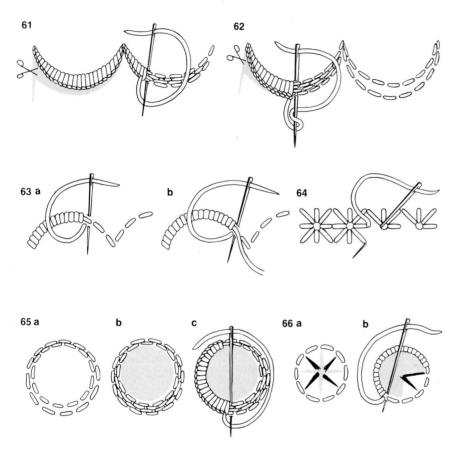

This sampler is worked with linen thread. A closer effect is obtainable with cotton thread

Buttonhole Stitch and Overcast Stitch, Scallops and Eyelets

61. *Scallops*. Work the outline with Running Stitch. Pad as required with either Running Stitch, Back Stitch, Stem Stitch or Chain Stitch. The buttonholing must be close and even. Finally, carefully cut away the fabric from the outside of the curve.

62. *Buttonhole Stitch* with an extra twist in the thread – the stitch used for tailor's buttonholes – here seen worked over a Running Stitch padding.

63. *Close Overcast Stitch*, (a) worked over Running Stitch, and (b) over a padding thread. Used in *broderie anglaise*.

64. *Algerian Eye Stitch*. The stitches that are worked outward from the center point form an eyelet when drawn tight.

65. *Buttonhole Stitch Eyelets*. Work rows of Running Stitch around the marked shape, adding rows of padding where necessary. Clip away the fabric to form a hole and work an edging of close buttonholing.

66. *Eyelet Holes*. For small holes, the fabric is pierced with a stiletto. For larger ones, the fabric is clipped into little points, which are turned inwards. See Figure 63 for finishing details.

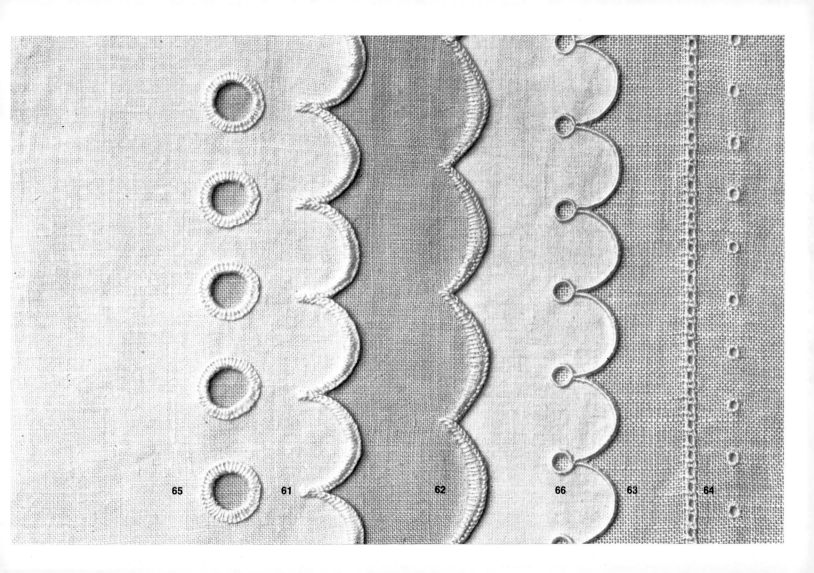

65   61   62   66   63   64

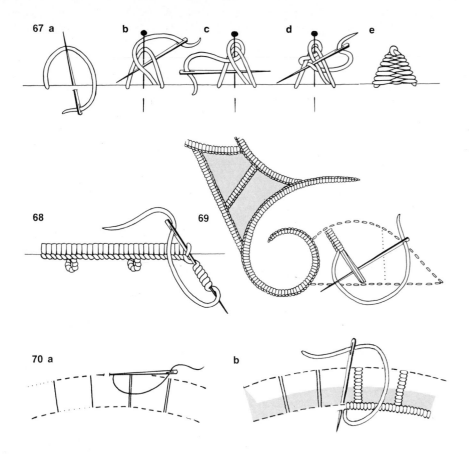

Picot Edgings, Venetian, and Richelieu Work

67. *Woven Picots* are worked more or less like darning, around a supporting pin.

68. *Bullion Picots* in conjunction with *Close Buttonholing*. Insert the needle into the upper part of the last Buttonhole Stitch. Twist the thread onto the needle, hold the thread firm and draw the needle through. The picot is secured by the next buttonhole stitch.

69. *Venetian Work*. Work the outlines in Running Stitch, covered by Buttonholing. The bars that are to cross the holes are worked at the same time as the Running Stitch. When the working is complete, the fabric to be removed is carefully cut away.

70. *Richelieu Work*. The Running Stitch and the threads forming the bars are worked at the same time, alternately from side to side. The two long stitches so formed are the foundations for the bars. Clip the fabric and turn it in. Overcast both edges and bars. The bars can be strengthened with an extra thread.

This sampler is worked with linen thread, although cotton produces a closer effect

70

69   68   67

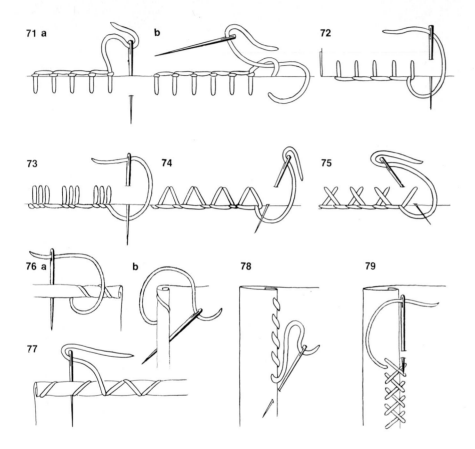

Hems

71. *Hedebo Buttonholing* is usually worked from the left. It should be close for buttonholes, more open for other kinds of edges.
72. *Open Buttonhole Stitch* (Blanket Stitch) over a turned-up hem.
73. *Spaced Buttonhole Stitch.*
74. *Closed Buttonhole Stitch.* This can be varied by, for example, taking three stitches from one point. To keep the oblique stitches in place, it is best either to bring the needle up through the edge of the fabric, or to take the right sloping stitch up through the previous loop.
75. *Crossed Buttonhole Stitch.*
76. *Rolled Hem.* This hem is rolled as it is worked. It can be worked vertically or horizontally, in a matching or a contrasting color.
77. *Rolled Hem* with double whipping.
78. *Hemming.*
79. *Herringbone Stitch.*

Buttonholing is seen here as a hem finish, but it can be used just as effectively as pure decoration

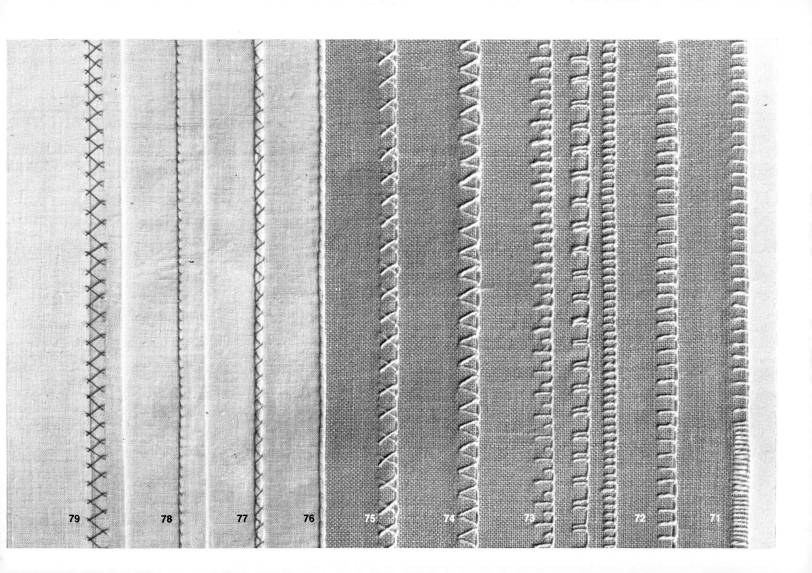

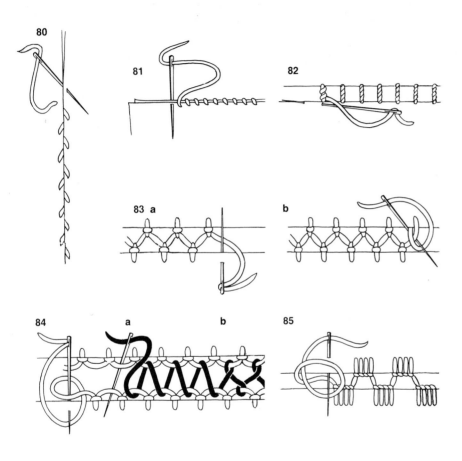

Overcasting and Insertion

80. *Fishbone Stitch* used to join pieces of fabric edge to edge is an extremely old form of seam. It can be worked either open or close.

81. *Overcasting* two pieces of cloth together, one on top of the other.

82. *Bar Insertion*, a very common method of joining fabrics. It is worked from either right or left, with one or more overcast stitches to each bar.

83. *Knotted Insertion Stitch.*

84. *Laced Insertion Stitch.* This will be firmer if as at (b) the needle is brought out behind the working thread.

85. *Buttonhole Insertion Stitch*, with one or more stitches to each side. Plain buttonholing can be used or, as here, tailor's buttonholing.

It is easier to maintain an even distance between the two edges to be joined if the fabric is firmly mounted on paper. These stitches can be worked in a matching or a contrasting color

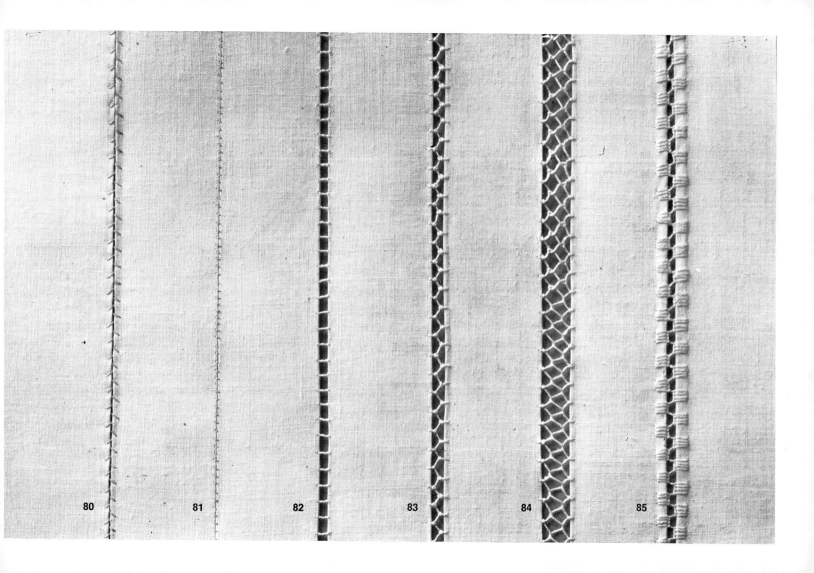

80   81   82   83   84   85

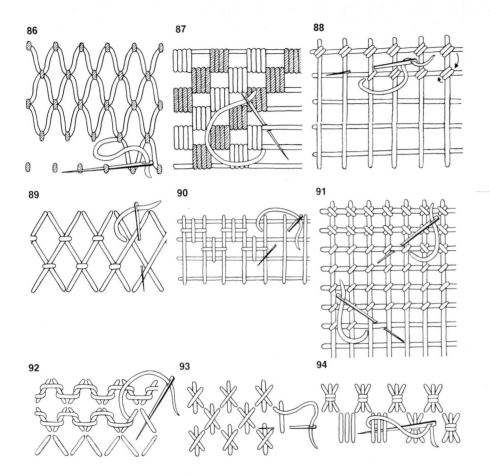

Fillings Couched and Overcast

86. *Cloud Filling Stitch*, threaded in a zigzag between rows of small stitches.
87. *Satin Stitch Blocks* worked over parallel laid threads to give a chequered effect. Tiny stitches may be taken into the ground fabric to keep the pattern firm.
88. *Couched Filling*. The long threads are fastened where they cross with small double stitches (see Figure 91 for the needle in the reverse direction).
89. *Couched Filling* of long diagonal threads, secured with small stitches.
90. Here a network of long threads is secured in alternate squares with upright crosses.
91. Worked like Figure 88, but with the couching stitches crossed.
92. *Whipped Wave Stitch*.
93. *Ermine Filling Stitch*.
94. *Sheaf Filling Stitch*.

The fillings that are worked 'loose', i.e. without entering the ground fabric, are done on closely-woven material inside traced shapes. A frame should be used. They are characterized by a network of laid threads held down with tiny stitches. The blocks of filling are often edged with stem stitch. There is endless scope for variation in materials and motifs

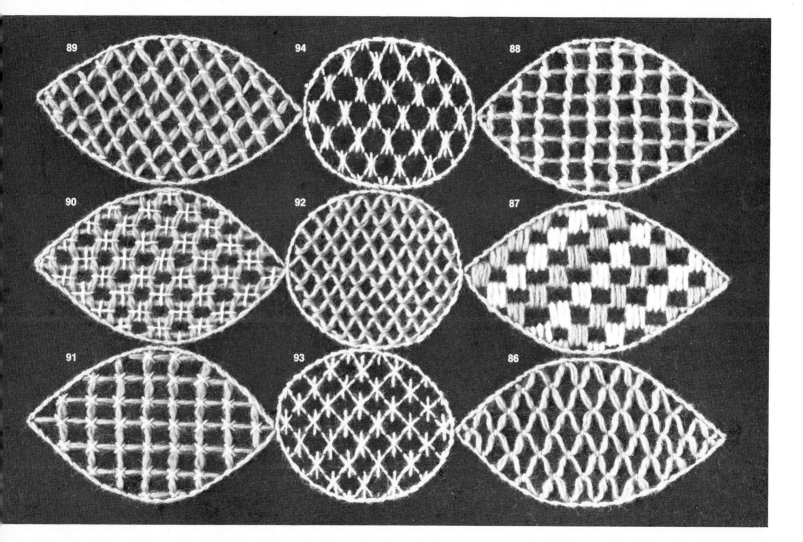

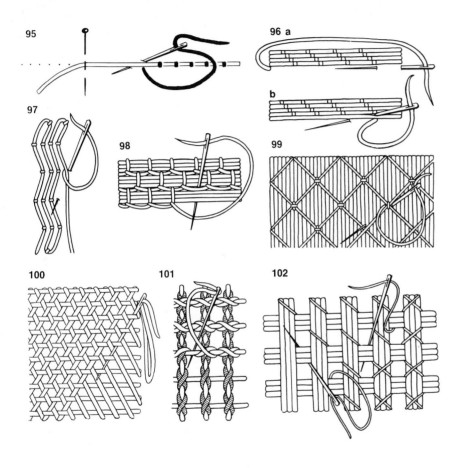

Couching and Laid Work

95. *Couched Thread* used for outlining. The thread to be couched is secured as the work proceeds.
96. *Bokhara Couching* as a filling. A long thread is taken across the space and couched down.
97. *Couched Thread* laid in a zigzag and secured as the work proceeds.
98. *Laid Work.* Three threads in Surface Satin Stitch, for example (see Figure 46), tied down with Buttonhole Filling.
99. *Laid Work.* The ground threads are worked as in Figure 98 or, if preferred, in two trips, the spaces between alternate threads left on the first trip being filled in on the second, to give a closer ground. Couch down the intersecting diagonals with fine thread.
100. *Honeycomb Filling Stitch.* Lay threads in two directions. Weave back and forth along the third.
101. Lay the threads and fasten them with Double Whipping.
102. Bundles of laid threads, fastened with woven crosses.

A number of these stitches are especially suitable for gold work, but they can also be carried out in other materials; here, wools

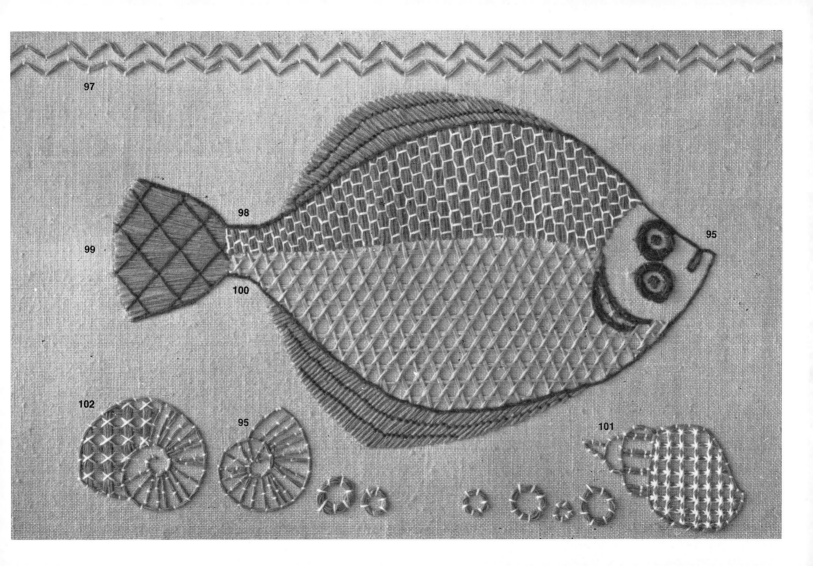

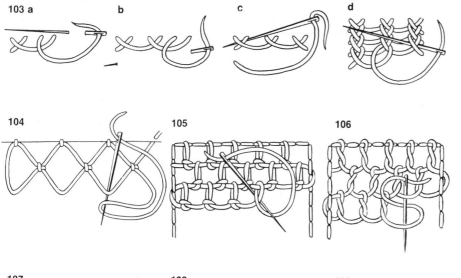

Lace Stitch Fillings

103. *Ceylon Stitch* should not be used over too wide a space, as the working is always in one direction with a long return thread on the wrong side.

104. *Filet*, here worked from the edge of a hem in *Knot Stitch*.

105. *Knotted Buttonhole Filling*, here used in a square, bounded with Back Stitch.

106. *Lace Stitch Filling*.

107. *Open Buttonhole Filling*.

108. *Open Buttonhole Filling* worked alternately singly, and paired, from the edge of a hem.

109. *Knotted Buttonhole Filling* and *Open Buttonhole Filling* in alternate rows.

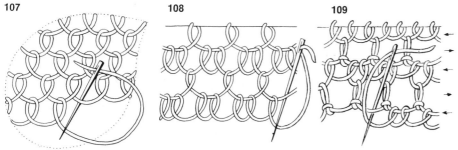

In coarse materials, and as detached fillings on a fabric ground, the old lace fillings, so much in demand in the past, can be brought to life again. This sampler shows several combinations. Some of the fillings are worked inwards from the marked edges of the circles, others outwards from a gently-curved line

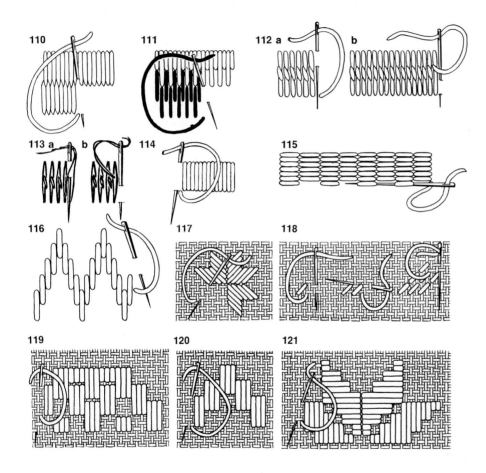

Satin Stitch, Roumanian Stitch, Florentine Stitch, Darning

110. *Encroaching Satin Stitch.* Insert the needle between the stitches of the previous row.

111. *Brick Stitch.* When it is worked in irregular shapes and with color variations, it is known as *Long and Short Stitch.*

112. *Roumanian Stitch.*

113. *Anundsjö Work.* This is worked like Figure 112, but with double thread. It is used as a leaf filling in Swedish folk embroidery.

114. *Satin Stitch* in a rectangle. The stitches on the right side lie parallel with the weave.

115. *Double Running.*

116. *Florentine Work.* Straight stitches, rising and falling over four threads.

117. *Satin Stitch* worked obliquely.

118. *Reversed Faggot Stitch*, here, three rows. (Figure 174 shows it worked in two rows.) Often used in conjunction with Satin Stitch.

119–121. *Satin Stitch* worked over counted threads, with the weave of the fabric.

This sampler is worked over counted threads

36

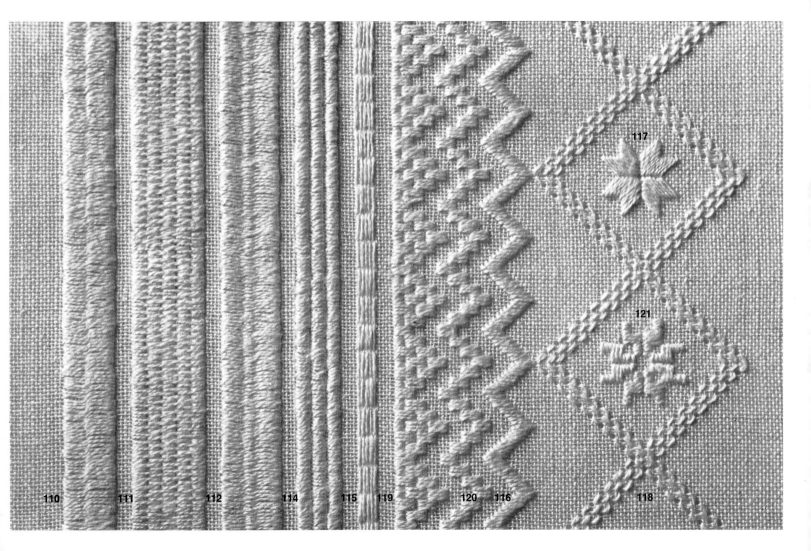

110 111 112 114 115 119 120 116 117 121 118

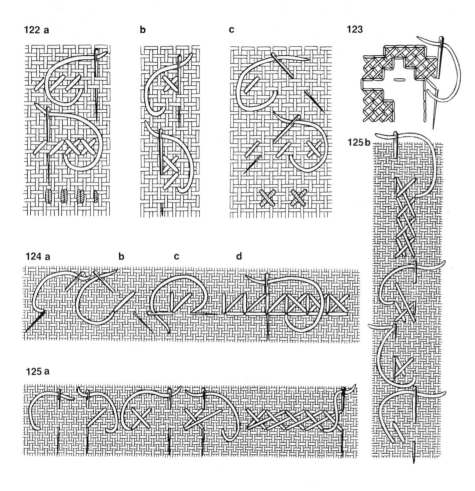

122 a   **b**   **c**   **123**

125 b

124 a   **b**   **c**   **d**

125 a

Cross Stitch, Long-armed Cross Stitch

122. *Cross Stitch*, worked over counted threads: (a) horizontally and (b) vertically, in which cases the stitches on the wrong side are vertical. In (c) the two strokes of the cross are worked on separate trips, in which case crosses are also formed on the wrong side.

123. *Assisi Work*. The blocks of Cross Stitch are edged with Holbein Stitch. The motif is usually left plain, and the Cross Stitches as background.

124. *Italian Cross Stitch.*

125. *Long-Armed Cross Stitch* can be worked in (a) horizontal and (b) vertical lines. The first and last stitches can, as in (b), be worked so as to maintain the parallels of the pattern. This stitch must not be drawn too tightly and is worked in a frame.

Cross Stitch may be used for both geometrical and naturalistic designs, with the background either left plain between the motifs or filled. The rows of Long-Armed Cross Stitch are an addition, worked vertically or horizontally to the demands of the pattern

38

125   122   124   125

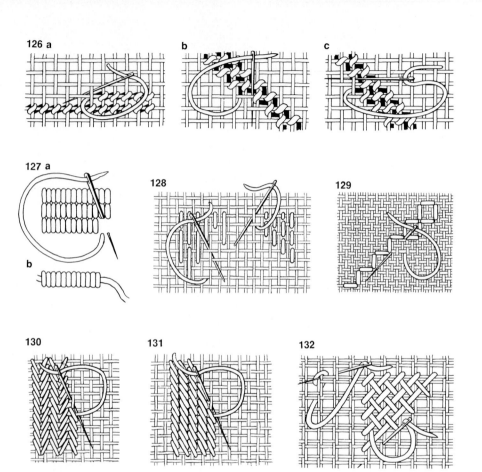

126 a   b   c

127 a   b

128

129

130

131

132

Gobelin Stitch, Petit Point, and various other Stitches for Canvas Work

126. *Petit Point* (*Tent Stitch*). Half a Cross Stitch taken over one thread, but under two on the way to the next stitch. Small areas can be worked either (a) horizontally or vertically; larger areas, (b) and (c), diagonally.

127. *Gobelin Stitch*, worked like blocks of geometrical Satin Stitch on coarse fabric or single canvas. It is taken over two or more threads; sometimes, as in (b), over an added padding-thread.

128. *Brick Stitch*, worked over an even number of threads, often two or four.

129. *Single Faggot Stitch* is often used in borders, but can also be a filling stitch.

130. *Satin Stitch*, worked diagonally. The stitch-length may be varied. (See also Broad Stem Stitch, Figure 15.)

131. Like Figure 130, but most often worked from the left.

132. *Web Stitch*. The long diagonal stitches are secured with short ones.

There is no need to leave the ground fabric plain outside the picture, as here. It can be completely filled

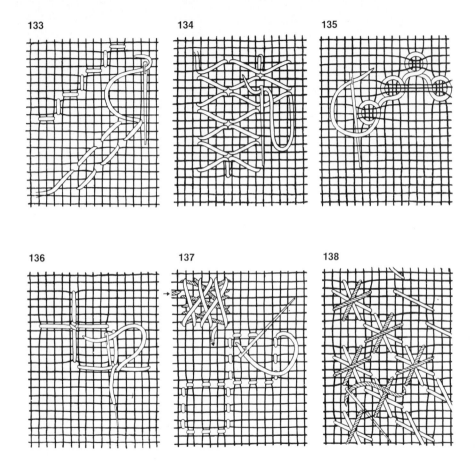

Drawn Fabric Work

133. *Single Faggot Stitch – Reversed.* Worked in diagonal rows as a filling-stitch. If the stitch is worked as in Figure 129, the threads on the right side lie with the weave.

134. *Wave Stitch Filling.*

135. *Indian Drawn Ground,* worked in small circles, over and under 3 × 3 threads.

136. *Greek Cross Filling,* here worked over 10 × 10 threads. Bring the needle up at one extremity of the cross, sew a pair of Buttonhole Stitches to complete the arms of the cross, and insert the needle into the first stitch.

137. *Cushion Stitch,* worked like crossed Back Stitch under a square of 6 × 6 threads. Can be used in both drawn fabric and shadow work, where it must be worked with looser stitches on finer, closer fabric.

138. *Chequer Filling Stitch.* Work an oblique line of Oblong Cross Stitch (white). To complete the stars, repeat the stitch in the opposite direction (grey).

This work is best done in a frame, and with linen thread. Draw the stitches tightly

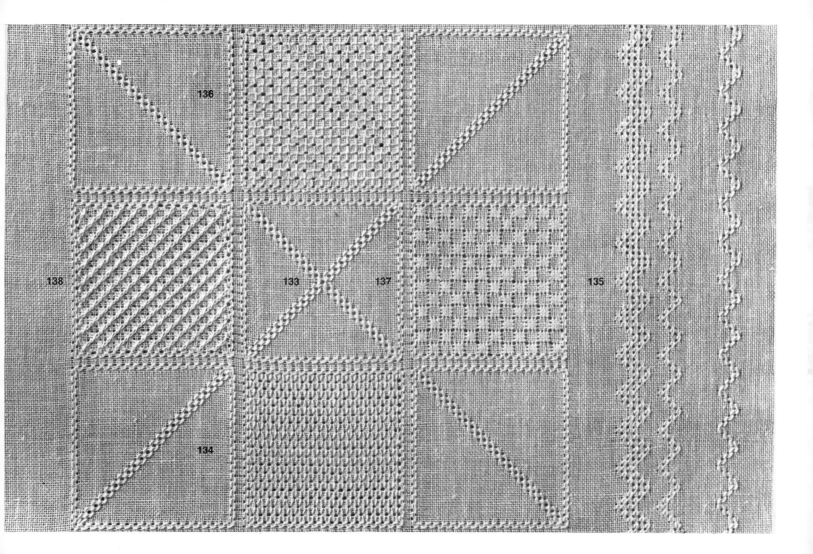

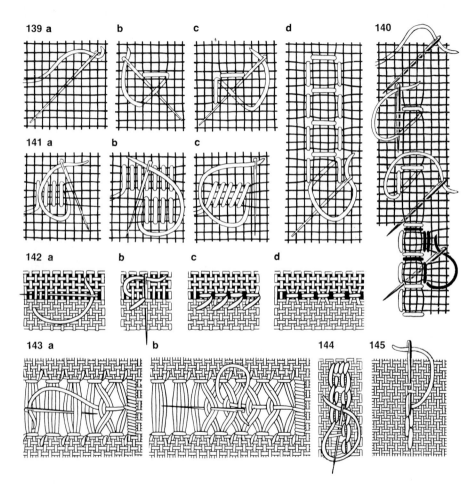

Drawn Thread Work, Hem Stitch

139. *Four-Sided Stitch*. On closely-woven material one thread can be withdrawn from each side.
140. *Four-sided Stitch Edging*. First work a row of half Four-sided Stitch. Then turn in the hem, and complete the stitch in a second row. The holes will be more pronounced if the second row is sewn double.
141. *Satin Stitch* drawn tight: (a) and (b) vertical stitches; (c) oblique stitches.
142. *Antique Hem Stitch* used here to secure a hem with the vertical stitch taken only through the folded edge. On close fabric, one or more threads can be drawn out. (d) shows the right side. This stitch can be used in appliqué work (see Figure 185).
143. A twisted border is worked like 142, except that both top and bottom are sewn from the right side and a thread brought through.
144. Bundles of threads held with *Single Feather Stitch*.
145. *Alternating Stem Stitch*. On close fabric, thread can be drawn out.

Other simple variations of hem stitching are Serpentine and Ladder Hems, illustrated at the bottom of the facing page

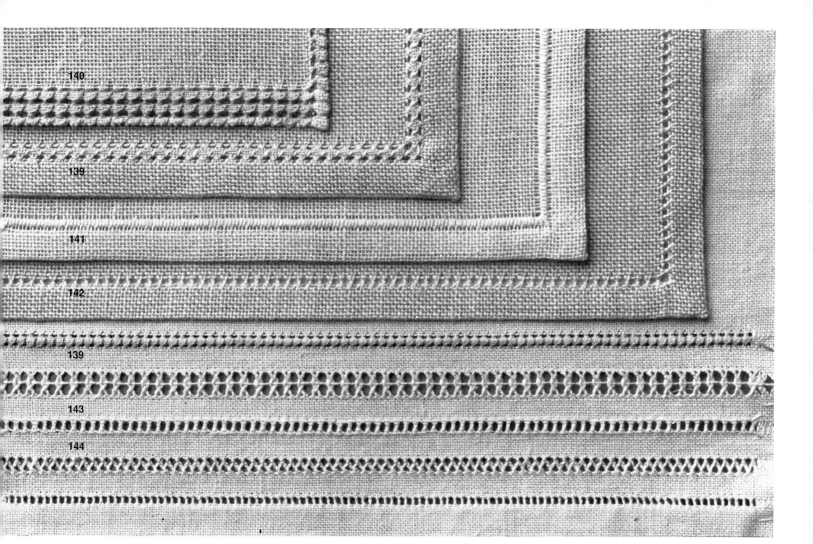

140

139

141

142

139

143

144

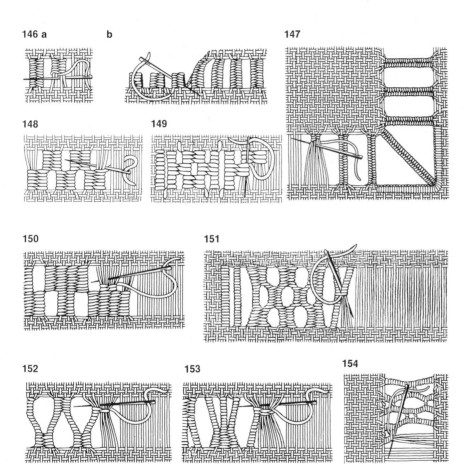

146 a   b   147

148   149

150   151

152   153   154

Needle Weaving and Woven Hem Stitch

Needleweaving is worked in darning, back and forth, from side to side, often with extra threads introduced into the work at the change of direction. The number of threads in each bundle must be suitable to the scale of the embroidery, in proportion to the thickness of the fabric.

146. *Needleweaving* as a hem finish.

147. Bars of *Needleweaving*. The corner is strengthened with overcasting or buttonholing. If the hole is too large, an extra bar is worked on long threads.

148. Bundles of threads woven together in pairs.

149. *Woven Hem Stitch*.

150. *Needleweaving* over four bundles.

151. If the width of the border is increased, the patterns of woven blocks and holes can be endlessly varied.

152. Like Figure 148, but with overcast bars in the centre.

153. *Needleweaving* with overcast bars.

154. *Overcast Bars*, knotted at intervals. These should be worked with thin thread.

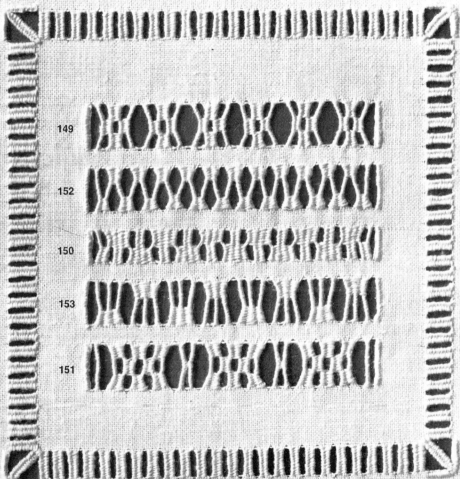

148 147 149 152 150 153 151 146

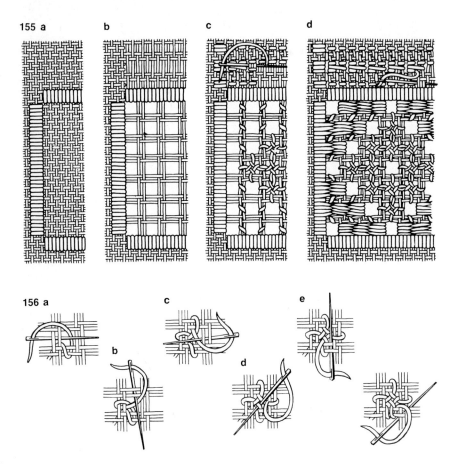

155 a   b   c   d

156 a   b   c   d   e

155. *Drawn Thread Work.* This style occurs in Amager Danish work. Count out the number of threads needed for the pattern. (a) Sew round the edge with Satin Stitch over 3–4 threads. (b) Clip and withdraw threads to form a regular square mesh. The threads in the borders are withdrawn as the work proceeds. (c) Overcast the ground threads in one direction only, working the vertical Lace Filling at the same time (see Figure 156). (d) Overcast the ground threads in the other direction and work the needleweaving. In this example, the overcasting is worked with one stitch for each bundle of threads in each direction, but two occur also. Many pieces of Amager work have a double row of Four-sided Stitch outside the Satin Stitch edging.

156. *Vertical Lace Filling* occurs in many types of drawn thread work.

In drawn thread work, endless variety is possible in the balance between the open and solid part of the pattern. It is best to use a frame

48

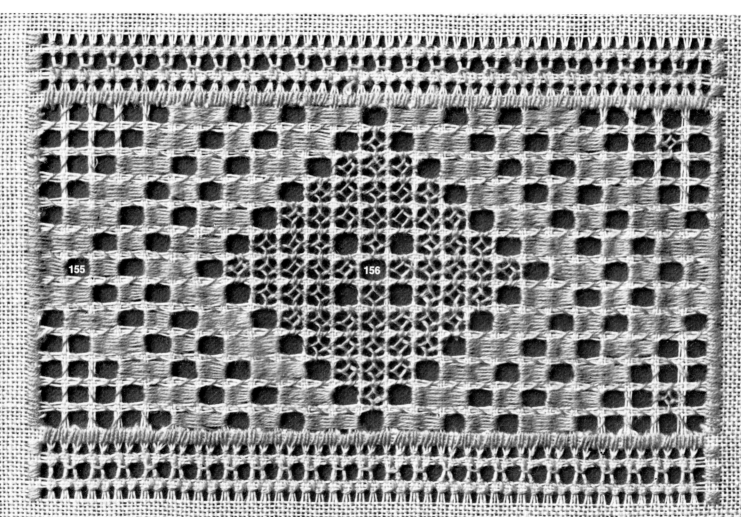

157   158 a   b   c

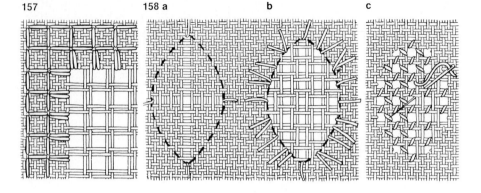

159   160   161

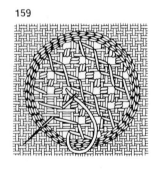 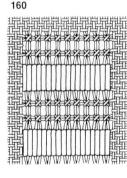 

157. *Drawn Thread Work* over counted stitches. This example is from Sjæland (Denmark). It is like Figure 155, except that it has only a single row of Four-sided Stitch, with two overcast stitches into each hole.

158. *Drawn Thread Work* in rounded motifs. Outline the shape with thin thread in a contrasting color. Now work from the back. (a) and (b) Clip and draw away the middle threads in each direction. Continue until the required mesh is obtained. If necessary, overcast the edge with fine thread, as invisibly as possible. Remove the outlining thread and turn back to the right side. (c) Overcast the ground threads, with one or more stitches to each bundle. This is used in white work.

159. Variation of *Overcasting*, the ground outlined in chain stitch.

160. A border of upright *Satin Stitch* and drawn thread work, overcast.

161. *Cut Work* drawn thread work with stepped edges. Motifs in cut work, like those in drawn thread work, can be sewn in darning and vertical lace filling.

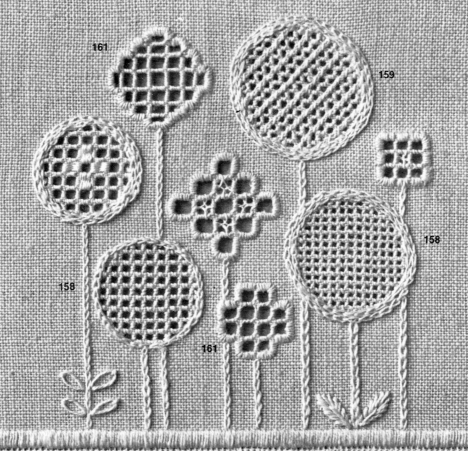

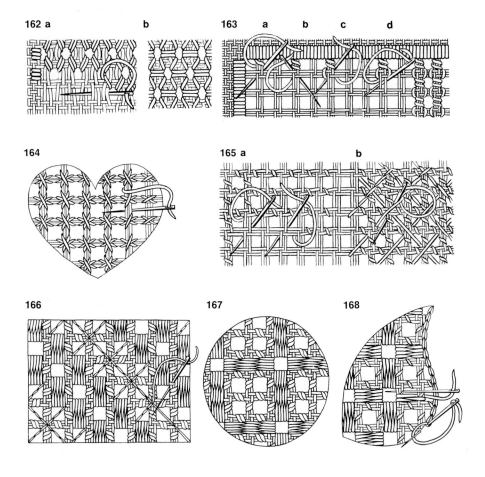

162 a b 163 a b c d

164 165 a b

166 167 168

Drawn Thread Work, White Work

162. *Wave Stitch Filling* (with the diagonal stitches double). In one direction only, draw out alternate pairs of threads. The reverse may also be used.

163. Rows of *Four-sided Stitch* separated by pairs of overcast stitches. Like the other stitches described in this section, this one can be used in both rectangular and rounded motifs.

164. *Overcasting* forming a double cross. Work all the crosses in one direction first, then in the other.

165. *Overcasting*, with (b) additional threads interwoven diagonally.

166. A ground composed of pairs of overcast stitches, darning and additional diagonal threads. Alternate pairs of threads were removed for the mesh.

167. A variation of 166.

168. Another variation. The edge is often finished with one or more rows of chain stitch.

These grounds often occur in white work in conjunction with Satin Stitch. This sampler is worked on rather fine fabric over more threads than in the instructions

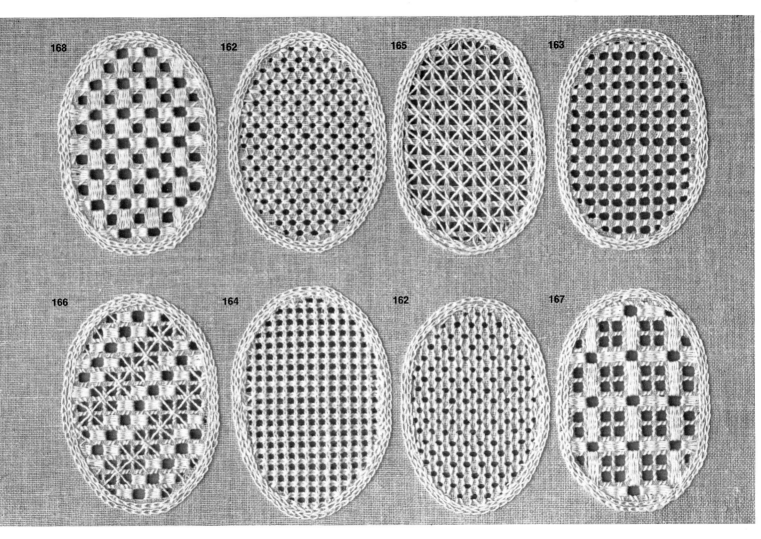

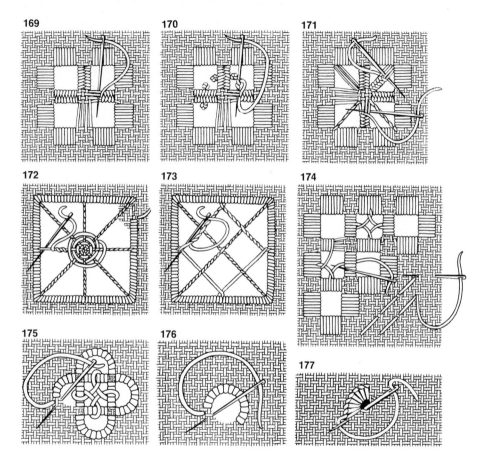

Hardanger Embroidery

169. *Satin Stitch* in rectangular blocks to mark the outer edges of the holes. Clip and draw out the threads. Use finer yarn for weaving the bars.

170. *Woven Bars* with *Picot*.

171. Additional diagonal threads, either two twisted or four worked in needleweaving.

172. *Spiderweb*. After the edge of the square has been outlined and overcast, the ground fabric is clipped away. Added threads form a single or a double cross, reinforced with overcasting. The arms of the cross are held together with darning.

173. A mesh of additional threads, twisted round each other.

174. Like Figure 169, but with overcast instead of woven bars. *Vertical Lace Filling* is typically found with both woven and overcast bars. Bands of reversed Faggot Stitch are commonly used to divide the field.

175. The two central threads in each direction are clipped and drawn out. A stiletto is used to extend each side of the resulting square.

176. A stiletto hole, overcast.

177. *Buttonhole Eyelets*.

Drawn thread work is very often done on linen with linen thread, but Hardanger can also be worked with mercerized thread on a double-woven cotton fabric

170   171   174   171   169

173   174   174

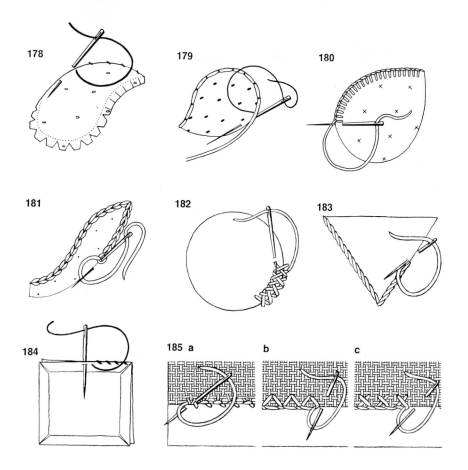

Appliqué and Seams

178. *Appliqué*. Those not wishing to work entirely free-hand can transfer the design on to paper and on to the ground material. The pieces to be applied are cut out around the paper pattern, with the addition of seam allowance to be turned in. The edges are secured with small running stitches or with slip stitch, depending on whether decoration is to be added or not. It may sometimes be necessary to cut small notches in the seam allowance.

179. *Couched Thread* edging.

180. *Buttonholing*.

181. *Chain Stitch*.

182. *Close Herringbone Stitch*.

183. *Broad Hem Stitch*.

184. To join two pieces – oversewing on the wrong side.

185. Fabrics of contrasting weave joined here with (a) hemstitching, (b) and (c) two forms of buttonholing.

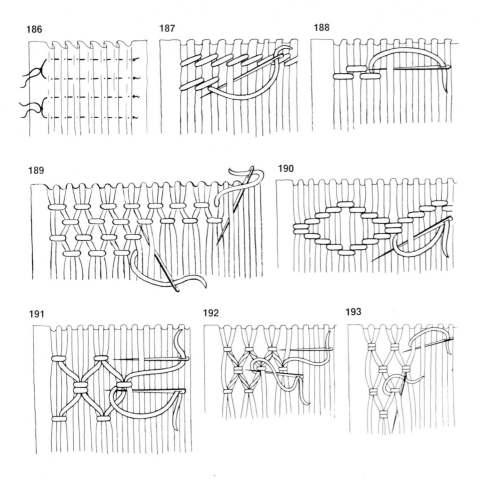

Smocking, Honeycombing

Unless check material is being used, it is necessary to mark lines of dots along the fabric grain on the wrong side. The distance between the dots should be about $\frac{3}{8}$ inch, rather more on coarse material, less on fine fabric. Graph paper is useful.

186. Pick up each dot on the running thread. Pull up the threads to the required width and knot them together, two and two.

187. *Stem Stitch* worked from either right or left.

188. *Alternating Stem Stitch.*

189. Worked like 188, except that an invisible oblique stitch through the fabric allows the rows of stitches on the right side to be more widely spaced.

190. *Stem Stitch* worked right and left into a zigzag pattern.

191. A variation using *Chevron Stitch* (see Figure 35).

192. *Honeycombing* with the working thread visible between the stitches. It is similar to 191 but worked over fewer gathers.

193. *Honeycombing* with the working thread hidden between stitches.

Smocking can be worked in a color to match the fabric, so that the relief effect predominates. This sampler is worked in contrasting colors

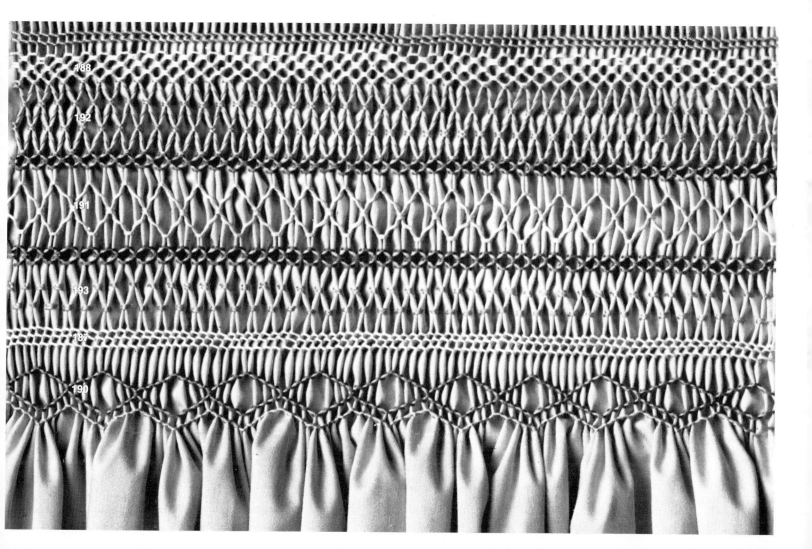

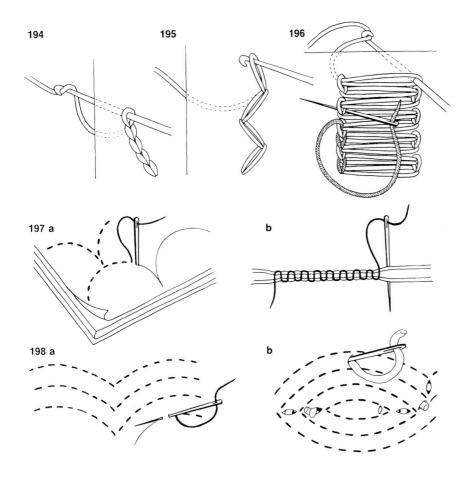

Tambour Work, Quilting

194. *Tambour Work* is done with a hook, but produces an effect very similar to Chain Stitch. It is pulled through fine fabric with a tambour-hook or a crochet hook. It must be worked over a frame.

195. *Zigzag Loops.*

196. The loops are pulled alternately from side to side along parallel lines. Overcasting secures them, and produces the appearance of a continuous Chain Stitch edge.

197. *Quilting.* Top and bottom layers with a padding of wool, cotton, or foam-rubber between. Work through all three layers with tiny Running or Back Stitches. Patchwork, an American folk-art, is usually quilted as well as appliquéd or pieced together from scraps.

198. *Italian Quilting.* The outer fabric, and the thin lining, on which the design is marked, are sewn together with small running stitches. Thick soft yarn, especially made for the purpose, is drawn between the layers, from the back.

This kind of embroidery gives a pronounced light-and-shade effect

194
195
196

197

198

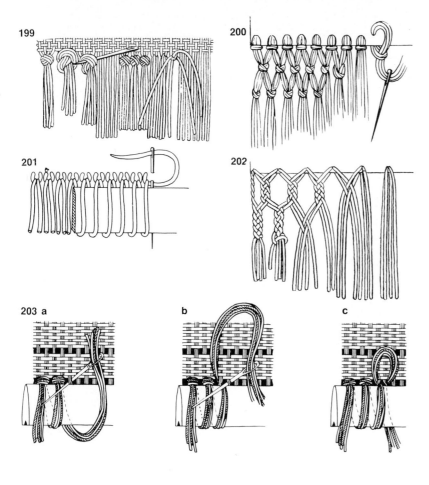

Fringes, Pile and Rya

199. *Knotted Fringe* made of the unravelled threads of the fabric itself. If larger knots or a closer fringe are wanted, extra threads can be added, fastened firmly in among the fabric threads before the knots themselves are formed. The knots can be made to lie neatly along the edge with the help of a needle.

200. *Fringe Knotted on,* then knotted further to form a pattern.

201. *Knotted Pile,* for fringing or filling.

202. *Plaited Fringe* using four threads. The end of each plait is secured with a knot.

203. *Rya Work* is done on special rya canvas, with or without a gauge. The loops may be cut unevenly, to give the effect of a pile.

These fringes can be knotted from the threads of the fabric itself or from added threads, no matter which method is applied here

62

199   200   201   202

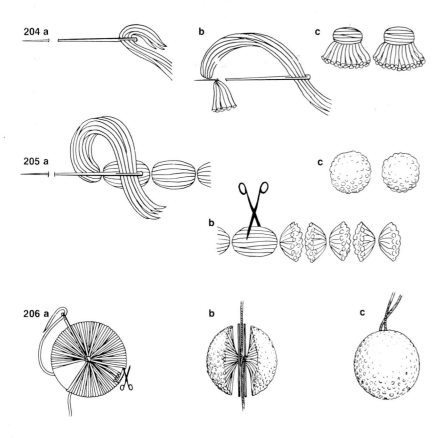

Pompons

204. *Single Knotted Stitch*. With a number of threads in the needle, sew small stitches as for Rya work. Cut the threads after each complete stitch.

205. For a line of pompons, work rows of Running Stitch with several threads in a coarse needle. Clip each stitch across the center, and bring up the pile with steam.

206. Free-hanging *Pompons*. These are worked over two discs of cardboard with holes in the center. If the pompons are to be dense, like those in the photograph, the holes must be quite large. Work round and round, one loop at a time, until the hole is filled. Clip round the edge, and tie a strong thread between the discs before they are pulled off. Neaten with scissors and sew on firmly.

Embroidery incorporating pompons is suitable for cushions and bedspreads

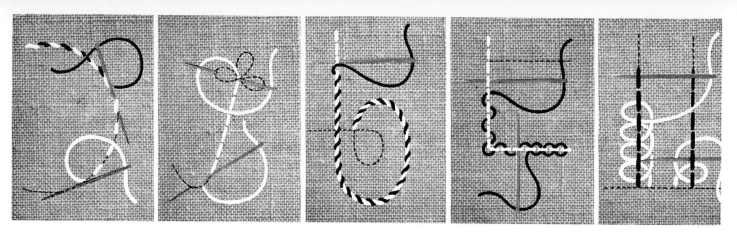

**Running Stitch
and Double Running**

**Whipped Back
Stitch**

**Threaded Back
Stitch**

**Pekinese
Stitch**

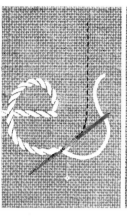
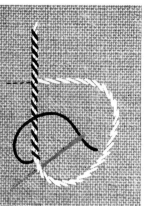
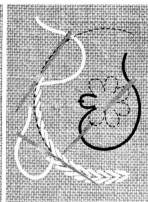
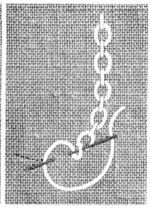
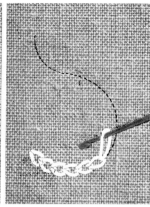

Stem Stitch

Whipped Stem Stitch

Stem Stitch and Outline Stitch with Fly Stitch

Cable Chain Stitch

Tambour work through the fabric

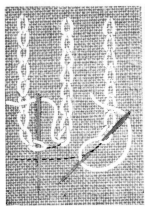

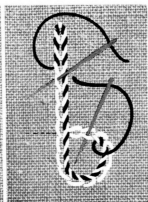
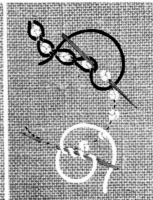

Chain
Stitch

Whipped Chain
Stitch

Variation of
Whipped Chain
Stitch

Chain Stitch
over French
Knots

Square Chain
or Open Chain
drawn into
sheaves

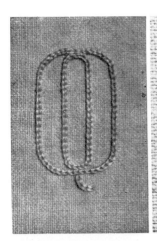

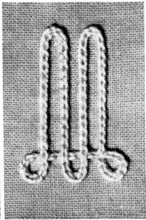

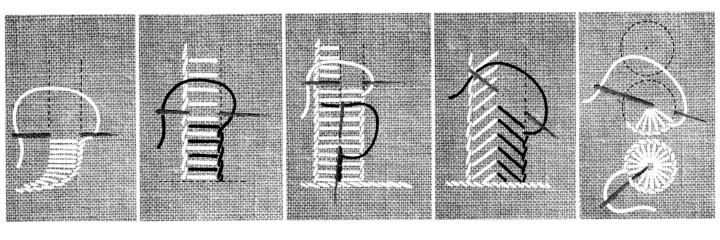

Buttonhole
Stitch

Double
Buttonhole
Stitch

Double row of
Buttonhole Stitch
with Stem Stitch
between

Single
Feather
Stitch

Buttonhole
Stitch
wheel

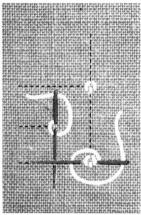

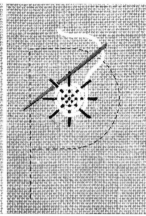

Bullion Knots

Tiny Detached Chains as Knots; may also be worked double

Couched threads and French Knots

Woven Spider Web Stitch

Seed or Dot Stitch powdering inside an outline

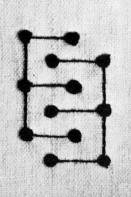
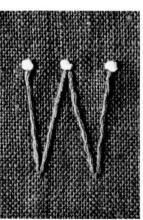

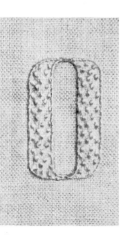

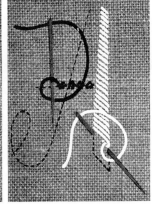
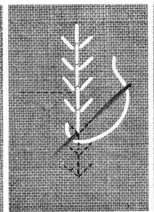

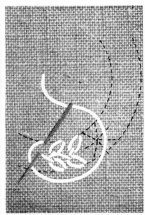

Coral Stitch. The
Flower in two versions
of Fly Stitch

Coral Stitch and
Rope Stitch

Fly
Stitch

Feathered
Chain Stitch

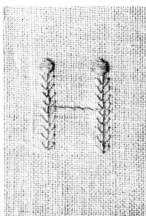

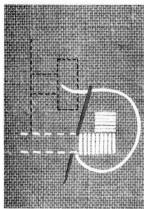

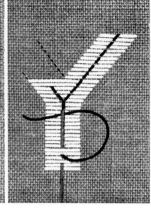

Geometric Satin Stitch, over a Running Stitch outline

Back Stitch worked over Satin Stitch

Alternate rows of Satin Stitch and Back Stitch

Satin Stitch edged with Stem Stitch

Satin Stitch worked in two directions

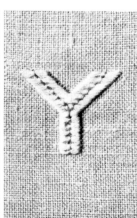

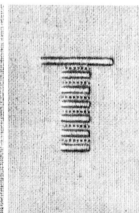

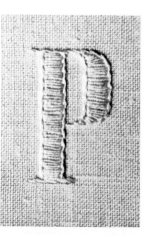

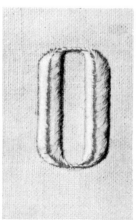

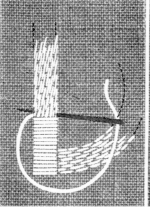
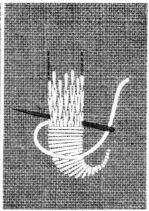
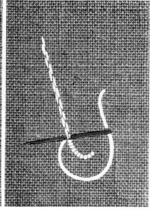

Surface Satin Stitch	Satin Stitch padded with Stem Stitch or Running Stitch	Satin Stitch padded with Split Stitch or Chain Stitch	Padding of one or two rows of Running Stitch, overcast	Eye Stitch

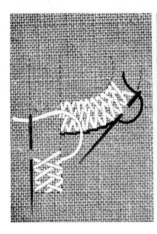

Closed Herringbone
Stitch with a Stem
Stitch edge

Shadow work
(reverse of closed
Herringbone Stitch)

Couching used
as an outline

Laid threads tied down
with Stem Stitch

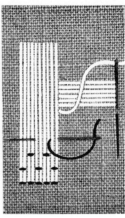

Laid threads tied down
with tiny Back Stitches

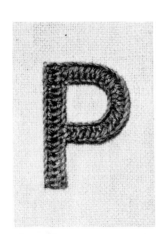

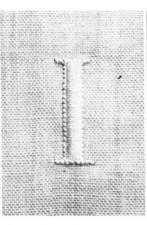

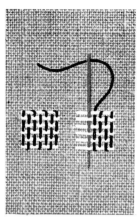

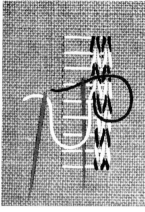

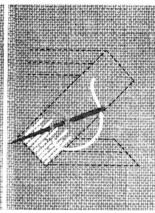

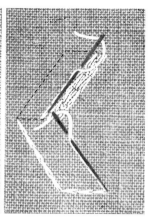

Surface Darning

Chequered Chain Band

Long and Short Stitch with Whipped Stem Stitch edge

Long and Short Stitch, and Stem Stitch outline

Split Stitch as outline and as filling

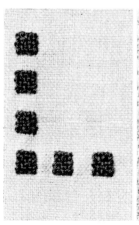

Index

The numbers refer to pages